Inflation-Protection Bonds

Understanding Structure and Implementing Strategies

Inflation-Protection Bonds
Understanding Structure and Implementing Strategies

John B. Brynjolfsson

Anthony L. Faillace

WILEY

ISBN 1-883249-22-8

Printed in the United States of America.

10 9 8 7 6 5 4 3 2 1

To Our Parents

About the Authors

John B. Brynjolfsson, a Vice President and Portfolio Manager for Pacific Investment Management Company, joined the firm and the fixed income portfolio management team in 1989. In addition to managing the PIMCO Real Return Bond Fund, he has been instrumental in the development of the firm's investment analytics. His previous investment experience includes consulting for Charles River Associates, analyzing arbitrage opportunities for JP Morgan Securities, and teaching finance at the University of Massachusetts. Mr. Brynjolfsson holds a bachelor's degree in physics and mathematics from Columbia College, and a master's in finance and economics from the M.I.T. Sloan School of Management.

Anthony L. Faillace, a Vice President and International Product Manager for Pacific Investment Management Company, joined the firm in 1994 from a consultant position at Deloitte and Touche. Previously, he was associated with The First Boston Corporation and worked as an international business consultant in Europe and Asia. He holds a BA in economics from the University of Texas and a Master of Management degree from the J.L.Kellogg Graduate School of Management, Northwestern University.

Table of Contents

Preface

Why do we find inflation-protection bonds interesting? We believe that this market will be big and immature. In other words full of opportunities. These opportunities are denominated in the billions of dollars.

First comes supply: it will be large. The largest issuer of debt in the world, the U.S. Treasury, has a great incentive to issue as many of these bonds as the market will bear — $50, $100, $500 billion, or even $1 trillion over the next 5 to 10 years. The more it issues, the better the Treasury matches its liabilities to its assets.

On the other side of the equation you have investors. First will be the tactical investors. Tactical investors act as a back stop, absorbing essentially unlimited supply of Inflation-Protection Bonds (IPBs) — if the yield is high enough. These investors will not pay for inflation protection, but they will buy the bonds if they get paid for assuming the inflation protection. And the Treasury is willing to pay for inflation protection.

Strategic investors will also purchase bonds. Strategic investors are those investors who have exposure to the ravages of inflation — which means just about everyone. These investors will be the big winners in this billion dollar endeavor. Strategic investors "should" be willing to pay for inflation protection, but at first they may not have to. Later, a balance will be struck, where some of the benefit of the program will accrue to the Treasury, and some will accrue to strategic investors.

It is rare for opportunities of such a magnitude to arise in financial markets. But in the past financial market innovation has created opportunity for those willing to shepherd the innovation process along.

We would like to thank a number of people for making this book possible. First we thank those individuals within Pacific Investment Management Company that have enabled us to undertake this effort. These individuals include William Gross, John Hague, and Brent Harris. We would also like to thank a number of other individuals who also contributed to our knowledge and helped us develop our thoughts. These people include Roger Anderson (U.S. Treasury), Erik Brynjolfsson (MIT), Bill Cullinan (PIMCO), Chris Dialynas (PIMCO), Jane Howe (PIMCO), John P. Matthews (Merrill Lynch), Barbara Moore (SEI Capital Resources), Ivor Schucking (Strong Capital), and Ellen Racklin (IBJ).

Chapter 1

What Are Inflation-Protection Bonds

Acute inflation brought an organized protest by laborers, who refused to work. And so 3,000 years ago, in the year 1170 B.C., the Egyptian necropolis of Thebes witnessed the first historically recorded strike.[1] Inflation it seems, has been with us as long as money itself.

In a testament to ingenuity, investors' antidote to inflation — Inflation-Protection Bonds[2] (IPBs) — are not a new concept either. In ancient Mesopotamia, some 1,000 years before Egypt's heyday, warehouse receipts referencing quantities of grains and other goods, in effect IPBs, were traded in a secondary market, and in some ways preferred to the currency of the day.[3]

IPBs are fundamentally different from nominal bonds and constitute a distinct asset class. IPBs preserve and grow purchasing power. In contrast, traditional bonds preserve legal currency, or what James Grant has called "Money of the Mind."[4] As such, IPBs certainly have appeal for institutions that want to diversify risk and thereby increase the efficiency[5] of their asset allocation. Modern portfolio theory suggests that IPBs help accomplish these goals. However, experiences in other countries suggest that the perennial drivers of financial markets, fear and greed, determine demand for these bonds as much as modern portfolio theory. Institutional and retail owners of

---

[1] James Trager, *The People's Chronology* (New York: Henry Holt and Company, Inc., 1994).
[2] "Inflation-Protection Bonds" is a term used by United States Secretary of the Treasury Robert Rubin. We use it, and the term IPBs, generically throughout this chapter. Other terms describing the same concept include "TIPS," "TIIS," "Inflation Index Linked Bonds," and "Real Return Bonds."
[3] Glyn Davies, *A History of Money* (Cardiff: University of Wales Press, 1994).
[4] James Grant, *Money of the Mind* (New York: Farrar, Straus, Giroux, 1992) is a book that more than catalogs the monetary history of the United States.
[5] Efficiency in the sense of being closer to the efficient frontier.

IPBs frequently express a view that inflationary pressures will surface or that a defensive alternative to riskier financial assets is needed.[6]

Inflation protection, or generating a predetermined real return in all monetary scenarios, is accomplished by indexing principal to a price index, such as the Consumer Price Index (CPI). At the time of issuance the IPB's principal is 100%, just as is the case for traditional bonds. Over time the principal value of the IPB is adjusted as the price index changes, keeping the principal constant in real terms. The coupons are also indexed, indirectly, because the coupon cash flow received by the investor is equal to the numerical product of the fixed percentage coupon rate and the indexed principal amount. Exhibit 1 illustrates how this works given some simplifying assumptions.

Regardless of the reason for their appeal, IPBs are a fundamental type of investment security. And with the January 1997 auction by the U.S. Treasury, they are the newest asset class in the U.S. financial market.

Exhibit 1: Cash Flow of IPBs

The cash flows of IPBs generate a nominal yield equal to the product of the real rate at the time of purchase and the inflation rate realized over their lifetime. For example if the real rate is 3.5% and realized inflation is 3% then:

$$\text{Nominal Yield} = (1 + \text{Real Yield}) \times (1 + \text{Inflation Rate}) - 1$$
$$= (1.035) \times (1.03) - 1 = 6.61\%$$

	Purchase	First Coupon	Last Coupon	Principal	Return
Date	1997	1998	2007	2007	2007
Real $ Cash Flow	(1,000)	35.00	35.00	1,000	3.50%
CPI	100.0	103.0	134.4	134.4	3.00%
Nominal $ Cash Flow	(1,000)	36.05	47.04	1,344	6.61%

Source: Pacific Investment Management Company

---

[6] This is somewhat ironic, since the valuation of IPBs is quite independent of any inflation forecast. Rather it is necessary to forecast inflation to determine the value of nominal bonds.

WHAT IS COVERED

In this book, we explain how to manage the risks and returns of allocations to IPBs. Section I presents an overview of IPBs, the players who use them, and the policy issues which relate to them. Section II covers strategic and structural issues from a more technical perspective. Section III explores methods of obtaining investment exposure to this asset class through managed vehicles and direct purchases.

Section I

Overview and Players

Chapter 2

A Brief History of IPBs

IPBs are conceptually so fundamental that it is certainly possible that they pre-dated nominal bonds, or even pre-dated coins. In essence, the buyer of these bonds is simply "storing" a basket of goods for consumption in the future. In the United States, IPBs date back to the birth of the nation: IPBs were issued by the Colonies during the Revolutionary War. In 1780, the state of Massachusetts created debt inscribed as follows:

> Both Principal and Interest to be paid in the then current Money of said STATE, in a greater or less SUM, according as Five Bushes of *CORN*, Sixty-eight Pounds and four seventh Parts of a Pound of *BEEF*, Ten Pounds of *SHEEP'S WOOL*, and Sixteen Pounds of *SOLE LEATHER* shall then cost, more or less than *One Hundred Thirty Pounds* current money, at the then current Prices of Said ARTICLES.[1]

Since World War II, IPBs have been issued by more than 15 countries. A partial list of those countries is provided in Exhibit 1. As the exhibit suggests, IPBs are not strictly issued by countries experiencing run-away inflation. In fact, often countries seem to issue IPBs just as they are embarking on successful disinflationary initiatives. For example, in Iceland inflation from 1949 to 1954 averaged over 15% per year. In 1955, the year following the introduction of their IPBs, its recorded inflation rate fell to 0%.[2] The recording of a 0% inflation rate, however, did not toll the death bell for Icelandic IPBs. In fact, the Icelandic IPB market took hold, and in 1995 all of Iceland's long-term debt was inflation protected.

---

[1] Willard Fisher, "The Tabular Standard in Massachusetts History," *Quarterly Journal of Economics* (May 1913), p. 454.
[2] *Statistical Abstract of Iceland*, Table 12.5, page 150.

Exhibit 1: Post War Introductions of Indexed Bonds and Inflation Rates

Date	Country	Index	Inflation
1945	Finland	WPI	6.4%
1950	France	Equities, Gold	16.9%
1952	Sweden	CPI	2.0%
1955	Israel	CPI	12.3%
1955	Iceland	CPI	15.7%
1964	Brazil	WPI	69.2%
1966	Chile	CPI	22.2%
1967	Columbia	WPI	22.2%
1972	Argentina	WPI	19.7%
1975	United Kingdom	CPI	16.1%
1981	United Kingdom	CPI	14.0%
1985	Australia	CPI	4.5%
1989	Mexico	CPI	114.8%
1991	Canada	CPI	4.8%
1994	Sweden	CPI	4.4%
1995	New Zealand	CPI	2.8%
1997	United States	CPI	3.0%

CPI: consumer price index; WPI: wholesale price index; Inflation: in year prior to introduction except Iceland, for which the prior 5-year average inflation is reported.
Source: John Y. Campbell and Robert J. Shiller, "A Scorecard for Indexed Government Debt," NBER Working Paper # 5587, May 1996. © 1996 John Y. Campbell and Robert J. Shiller

By issuing IPBs, government officials make clearer their commitment to maintaining a low level of inflation. The willingness of a government issuer to assume the financial risk of inflation is a powerful signal to the market place regarding future governmental policy. The attitude of officials who favor issuing IPBs is best characterized by Donald T. Brash, Governor, Reserve Bank of New Zealand. In a recent speech he explained his support for IPBs as follows:

The only "cost" to Government is that, by issuing inflation-adjusted bonds, it foregoes the opportunity of reducing, through inflation, the real cost of borrowing… Since

Government has no intention of stealing the money invested by bondholders, foregoing the right to steal through inflation hardly seems a significant penalty.[3]

This rhetoric has been accompanied by monetary and fiscal policy action that the financial markets have applauded. In particular, New Zealand has adopted a singular, and highly transparent, monetary policy goal of eliminating inflation. In addition it has adopted a fiscal goal of not just eliminating current fiscal deficits, but of paying off the central government's past borrowings.

IPBs Issued by the United Kingdom

The United Kingdom's experience with IPBs represents the most notable example of a government issuing IPBs. Certainly the U.K. market for IPBs is the largest, but the program is also noteworthy in that it has saved the government significant revenues. The Bank of England geared up its issuance in the early 1980s, just as gilt investors were most skeptical of the government's inflation fighting ability, and as inflation was peaking.

A few years earlier, in 1975, the U.K. government issued non-marketable savings bonds with inflation protection. Popular with the elderly in the United Kingdom, the saving instruments came to be known as "Granny Bonds." In August of 1981, the government issued its first marketable IPBs[4] — with ownership restricted to non-taxable pension funds. The demand for IPBs among this group was substantial, which resulted in the government being able to sell the bonds with a meager real coupon of 2.0%. The relatively low real coupon was not surprising given the accelerating inflation environment of the United Kingdom during the 1970s and the resulting real underperformance of nominal asset classes during that decade. In fact, surveys conducted prior to the issuance suggested that many investors would have been willing to lock in 0%, or even negative real returns, simply to obtain contractual inflation indexation.[5]

---

[3] Donald T. Brash, "Monetary Policy and Inflation-Adjusted Bonds," *An Address to the New Zealand Society of Actuaries* (April 12, 1995).

[4] These are generally called index-linked gilts. "Gilt" is short-hand for "Gilt-Edged Stock," bonds issued by the government of the U.K.

[5] Andrew Roberts, "Index-Linked Debt" *A Presentation by UBS Bond Analyst Andrew Roberts at PIMCO* (August 1996).

In 1982, the tax issues associated with holding IPBs outside of tax-exempt pension accounts were addressed. Legislation in the United Kingdom exempted the inflation component of return from capital gains taxes. This was instrumental in creating a large retail clientele for these assets.

Another major step in the evolution of this market was taken prior to the election of 1983. With the threat of a potential Labour government victory in the air, the market's anxiety led the Conservative government to issue an IPB, which in a multi-layered play on words came to be known as the "Maggie Mays."[6] These were IPBs with an imbedded option exercisable after the feared election. The option allowed the holder to convert into a higher coupon nominal bond. The Thatcher government prevailed at the polls, and the disinflationary policies of the Conservative government initiated earlier in the 1980's continued. Not surprisingly, the conversion options of the "Maggie Mays" were almost universally exercised.

By the mid-1980s, inflation dropped substantially and the volume of IPB issuance by the U.K. government grew dramatically. Real yields increased from 2% to about 4%. Since then, the U.K. IPB market has continued to grow and real yields have generally remained between 3.5% and 4.5%. (See Exhibit 2.) IPBs issued by the U.K. government now comprise about 15% of all U.K. government debt outstanding.

The first 15 years of the market for index-linked gilts represented an extremely hostile environment for IPBs. In the United Kingdom, inflation dropped from 14% in 1982 to below 3% in 1996. This resulted in lower inflation adjustments for IPB holders. In addition, real yields increased from approximately 2% to 4%. This adversely impacted market prices and early buy-and-hold investors who locked in the low real yields for long terms. As a result, the nominal returns on index-linked gilts over this period were poor and substantially lower than those of traditional gilts.

However, even in this most hostile of environments the index-linked gilts performed quite well on a risk-adjusted basis. The 7.65% annualized nominal return they generated over this period was

---

[6] "Maggie Mays" could refer to the Margaret Thatcher's option to decide when to hold the election, the month the bonds mature or, to Liverpool's "Maggie Mae," famous for exploiting markets of a quite different type.

accompanied by a relatively low 6.59% annual standard deviation of nominal returns. By comparison, equities in the United Kingdom which thrived in the disinflationary environment, posted returns of 18.19%, but also suffered a higher standard deviation of returns at 15.76%.[7] (See Exhibit 3.)

Exhibit 2: History of Index Linked Gilt Yields

UK Index Linked History
(Real Yield)

Exhibit 3: Disinflationary Environment Returns and Risks

The Environment:	1981 "Monetary Despair"	1994 "Death of Inflation"
Inflation:	12.4%	2.6%
Real Rates:	2.5%	3.8%

The Result: (1981-1994)	Returns (Nominal Annualized)	Risk (Standard Deviation)
Equities:	18.2%	15.8%
Indexed Gilts:	7.6%	6.6%

Source: *Financial Times*, December 1981 to December 1994.

[7] The National Bank of New Zealand, *Inflation Linked Bonds: and New Zealand Guide*, February 1995. P. 45ff. Historical periods sited are 1982-1994.

It would be inaccurate to characterize the last 15 years experi-ence in the United Kingdom as a "worst" case scenario for IPBs. However, it is comforting to see how well IPBs performed in this hos-tile environment. Looking forward, it is reasonable to expect that if the environment changed and the inflation phoenix arose, we would find that the real return on equities would decrease and the real return on IPBs would increase. In such an environment, the two asset classes would no longer have comparable risk-adjusted returns. Rather IPBs would dominate equities by having both higher return and lower risk.

When IPBs were first issued in the United Kingdom, they were primarily intended to serve the needs of long-term savers, and even more so, pension organizations. As expected, these communities did purchase IPBs. And even though these investors experienced poor nominal returns in the 1980s and first half of 1990s, those who pur-chased the bonds for the purpose of locking in real returns achieved their objective. Since achieving real returns is a valid objective, there is still demand for IPBs in the United Kingdom.

Chapter 3

Real Interest Rates

Traditionally the yield of a default-free nominal bond ($\text{Yield}_{\text{Nominal}}$) is broken down into three components: the real interest rate ($\text{Yield}_{\text{Real}}$), expected inflation (Expected{Inflation}), and the inflation risk premium, (Risk Premium$_{\text{Inflation}}$). That is,

$$\text{Yield}_{\text{Nominal}}$$
$$= \text{Yield}_{\text{Real}} + \text{Expected}\{\text{Inflation}\} + \text{Risk Premium}_{\text{Inflation}}$$

The *real interest rate* is the market clearing yield of IPBs. Since the CPI can be thought of as a "basket" of goods which consumers purchase and use, IPBs can be viewed as bonds which are denominated in units of this basket of goods. Therefore, the real interest rate is the component of nominal yield which compensates market participants for deferring current consumption of a CPI basket in order to obtain more future consumption. On the producer side of the equation, the real interest rate is also the risk-adjusted real hurdle rate that producers must earn to justify borrowing.

Obviously the higher the real interest rate, the greater the incentive for a consumer to defer consumption, and the greater the disincentive for a producer to borrow capital. The market real interest rate balances these incentives. More formally, the real interest rate is the equilibrium rate of return between the inter-temporal transfer of consumption and real capital.

The *expected inflation* is that component of nominal yield which compensates investors for the expected erosion in purchasing power of money over time. Conceptually, this differs from the *inflation risk premium*, which is the component of yield demanded by the long-term lender and paid by the borrower to compensate for the *uncertainty* of nominal bond's real returns resulting from uncertain inflation. This inflation risk premium for long-term debt cannot be directly measured, but is thought to be in the range of 0.5% to 1.0% per annum for the U.S. market.

REAL INTEREST RATE STRUCTURE

These abstract concepts, real interest rates, expected inflation, and inflation risk premium, are not directly traded among market participants. But instruments that embody them are. The supply and demand relationships for the various securities evolve into an economic equilibrium that determines the prices of nominal bonds, floating-rate notes, IPBs, and other related instruments.

However, to the extent that there are inefficiencies, multiple market segments will evolve and reach equilibrium. In particular, observed real interest rates can and do differ across market segments. Differing values of expected inflation and inflation risk premiums will also exist across market segments. For example, the expected inflation necessarily depends upon the currency in which debt is denominated, and upon the monetary authority managing that currency. Similarly, inflation risk premiums will differ to the extent that volatility and participants' risk aversions differ across market segments.

OBSERVATION OF REAL INTEREST RATES

An historical record of real interest rate exists for countries that issue IPBs. These records can only be of partial help in understanding the return dynamics of IPBs, because of the relative brevity of the historical episodes covered. For example, the epoch covered by the U.K. IPB market, from 1981 to 1996, is one of secular disinflation, and is not representative of other secular environments. The data from other countries that issue IPBs are also limited, in terms of time span covered, and breadth of participants represented.

Rather than focusing on observed real interest rates obtained from the IPB market, a proxy for real interest rates is sometimes unadvisedly constructed by subtracting historical inflation from historical nominal bond yields. This proxy is often loosely called "the real interest rate." Even though such a proxy expands the data available for study, the data so introduced may incorporate as much noise as information into the analysis.

The problem is that historical inflation is not identically equal to inflation expectations. Survey data reporting the inflation "outlook," in theory should be more reflective of "market" expectations than historical inflation is, but such data are generally considered by financial economists to be even more suspect. Even if inflation expectations were known, substantial uncertainty as to the true real interest rate would still remain. This is because, in the absence of IPBs, the inflation risk premium remains as an unobservable quantity. So, the degree of uncertainty regarding the true level of real interest rates, even given well researched proxies, is large enough to detract from the analysis of real interest rate levels, and noisy enough to render any conclusions regarding real interest rate dynamics questionable.

Lastly, historical analysis, whether based on proxies for real interest rates or directly observed real interest rates, can only be used to provide context. Macroeconomic conditions never exactly repeat themselves in totality. Therefore, real interest rate models can never be tested as such.

These types of challenges are of course not unique to real interest rates, or IPBs; rather they universally characterize virtually all macroeconomic phenomena. Macroeconomics is not a hard science. However, if one were to compare the understanding of IPBs with other asset classes, one would likely agree that dynamics of IPBs are relatively well understood. As a comparison, the relationship of nominal bond yields to macroeconomic phenomena layers the complexity of real interest rate and inflation rate determination. Equity valuation, we would argue, is infinitely more inexact, and therefore focuses on fundamental analysis, statistical relationships, and the forecasts of market strategists.

In the end, those who are most able to synthesize all the available information relating to real interest rates will be the best prepared to benefit from the evolution of the IPB asset class.

Chapter 4

Market Participants

The market for IPBs is a global market of government and corporate issuers, institutional and retail investors, and proprietary and market making traders.

ISSUERS' PERSPECTIVE

IPB issuers are motivated by low real rates and low inflation adjustments. However, understanding issuers involves much more than simply exposing their basic motive of lowering financing costs. Ultimately, it involves exploring their approach to better achieving economic efficiency.

     The fact that issuers pay interest on capital raised through the issuance of IPBs is unexceptional. But the risk elimination and risk shifting that results from the inflation indexation is of keen interest. Economists' support for IPBs is strong because the bonds, through indexation, have the ability to extinguish inflation risk, and to transfer risk to those best suited to assume it. *IPBs extinguish risk by bringing together those issuers who have a positive exposure to rising inflation with those investors who have a negative exposure to rising inflation. IPBs transfer risk by allowing those investors who are most adversely impacted by inflation to purchase IPBs while leaving the riskier nominal bonds to those better suited to assume risk.* In both the extinguishing of risk and shifting of risk, IPBs create a win-win situation for issuers and investors.

     As the world's largest issuer of debt, the U.S. Treasury's success hinges on the success of the monetary authority in maintaining the integrity of the currency of the United States. Federal Reserve Bank officials and other economists have suggested that the "price discovery" role of IPBs contributes to better management of monetary policy.

17

In the past, a central banker's performance was often gauged by nominal yields on government bonds. Following the introduction of IPBs, real yields have also been utilized, but in a different way: real yields are subtracted from nominal yields resulting in a spread. The interpretation of this spread is straightforward; it directly implies what component of nominal bond yields is due to the risk of inflation.

This gives inflation hawks a powerful, if somewhat mechanical, weapon in their fight against a lax monetary policy. In particular, IPBs provide a direct measure of central bank performance. The political impact is substantial since this spread is a highly visible quantification of the increased governmental interest expense attributable to tolerating inflation.

Market veterans should be sure to reverse their intuition regarding central bank rhetoric in such an environment. Traditionally, central bankers are careful to support a strong bond market at every public opportunity in order to foster lower yields. In this way, not only do they lower governmental interest expense, they shed positive light on their own "inflation fighting" performance. However, central bankers do not shed positive light on their own performance by fostering lower yields on IPBs. In fact, central bankers would benefit with respect to this mechanical measure of their inflation fighting credibility by fostering *higher* yields on IPBs. In this way the spread between nominal yields and real yields is compressed and a lower "market implied" inflation forecast results.

Private Issuers

Traditional asset/liability management tends to emphasize a strategy of matching debt instruments with the usable life of assets: long-term debt is used to finance long-term assets, short-term debt is used to finance short-term assets. However, firms have come to recognize that the risk profile created by differences in the risk exposure of assets and liabilities may be as important as the maturity profile. Some have learned this only through direct experience.

For example, ever since the breakdown of the Bretton Woods fixed exchange rate agreement in the early 1970s, currencies have experienced substantial volatility. Treasurers of U.S.-based multinational firms were soon made acutely aware of any mismatches in the currency exposure of their assets and liabilities. In particular, when the dollar strengthened in the mid-1980s, foreign assets and revenues depreciated while the dollar-based liabilities appreciated. This resulted in substantial recognized and unrecognized losses for these global companies. More recently, Japanese multinationals suffered a similar consequence as the Japanese yen appreciated in early 1995.

In an environment of stable inflation, issuers' real-versus-nominal mismatches are often overlooked, just as currency mismatches were overlooked prior to the breakdown of Bretton Woods. But the impact of significant deflation on an issuer of nominal debt can be onerous. Even if a company maintains its unit sales, margins and real operating profits, the nominal cash flow generated by real assets decreases in a deflationary environment. This can make servicing nominal debt difficult, or even impossible.

Conversely, the impact of significant price inflation *seems* to be highly positive on an issuer of nominal debt. The entity's debt burden is "inflated" away. However, under closer scrutiny, characterizing the windfall as a gain glosses over the operating inefficiency of issuing nominal debt to finance real assets. Given such a scenario, a critical analysis might conclude that the company under-utilized its borrowing capacity.

A common perspective on the two scenarios shows that the problem is not one in which a company issues too much debt in a deflationary scenario or too little in an inflationary one. It is one in which a company issues nominal debt when "real" debt would better match the risk profile of its assets in both scenarios.

To some extent these risk profile matching qualities of IPB issuance can be accomplished through other types of debt vehicles. In particular, floating-rate debt indexed to LIBOR, prime, CDs, or other short-term interest rates can mitigate asset liability mismatches. These indices do tend to mirror shifts in the CPI, though not as well as IPBs do.

Prior to the issuance of the first U.S. Treasury IPB in 1997, there were a number of private inflation protected issues. In 1988, the Franklin Savings Association issued inflation protected CDs which were indexed to the CPI and "REALs" which were 20-year bonds that paid out their inflation accrual periodically in addition to a real coupon rate of 3%. Other corporate issuers include Anchor Savings Bank and JHM Acceptance Corporation.[1] However, without a reference real yield provided by a recognized U.S. benchmark, these issues have remained relatively obscure.

Public Issuers

Governments consider many of the same issues that private sector organizations consider when deciding to issue IPBs. Even though governments' greatest assets are intangible, the goal of matching assets with liabilities is still relevant. For example, the taxing powers of governments are an intangible asset, but they are certainly real. This partially explains why it is prudent for governments to assume the apparent risk of issuing IPBs as liabilities. However, governments are unique in their various roles as the sovereign entities, monetary authorities, and publishers of price indices.

Sovereign debt is either denominated in the issuer's domestic currency or in a foreign currency. The sovereign obviously has great, if not unlimited, flexibility to repay debt denominated in its own currency. It can devalue and therefore reduce the real value of its liabilities by simply increasing the money supply. As a result, the investment analysis of such debt de-emphasizes credit risk, and instead, focuses on the currency and interest rate risk of such debt.

In contrast, sovereigns have little or no flexibility in deciding how to repay debt denominated in foreign currencies. The analysis of such debt — for example Mexican government debt denominated in U.S. dollars — focuses almost exclusively on the probability and severity of credit problems. (Major industrialized countries generally issue debt denominated in their own currencies, although there are also examples of these governments issuing debt denominated in foreign currencies.)[2]

Sovereign issued IPBs are something of a hybrid between domestic currency debt and foreign currency debt. IPBs are denomi-

---

[1] Nigel H.M. Williams, et al, *Inflation Linked Bonds: A New Zealand Guide* (Wellington: The National Bank of New Zealand, February 1995), p. 17.

[2] For example, French government bonds, OATs, are generally denominated in French francs; however OATs denominated in European Currency Units (ECU) also exist. Italy is even more adventurous, issuing global bonds in a variety of currencies, based on demand relayed to the Italian authorities by a network of underwriters.

nated in the domestic currency of the sovereign. But simultaneously, IPBs mimic foreign currency denominated debt in certain respects. Specifically, since IPBs are protected against inflation, the sovereign's flexibility for devaluing their real value through currency debasement and inflation is largely extinguished. If the sovereign "prints money" to pay off its liabilities, the inflation indexation would adjust the principal value of the bonds upward to keep the IPBs' real value constant. The appendix to this book discusses a recent crisis of this nature involving sovereign debt indexed not to inflation, but to exchange rates.

INVESTORS' PERSPECTIVE

Investors may use IPBs for both strategic and tactical investment purposes. Strategic investments directly further core business goals. For example, a mandate designed to further asset/liability management and benchmarked against the Lehman Brothers Inflation-Linked Treasury Index would be a strategic investment.[3] Tactical investing is designed to harvest opportunities that arise out of transient circumstances and market dynamics. Implementation of tactical and strategic investment programs is covered later in this chapter.

Strategic Investors

Pensions, endowments, and other segments of the institutional investor community, as well as retail investors, can make significant strategic use of IPBs. In addition, foreigners, and foreign central banks in particular, may prove to be another group that generates strategic demand for IPBs. Traditional bonds are the most appropriate low-risk strategic asset to hold against nominal liabilities. However, many liabilities are "real"; that is, they increase if future price levels are higher. Examples include a pension plan's obligation to pay out benefits that are related to terminal salaries, an endowment's mandate to deliver educational or charitable services that are related to the real cost of operating facilities, and an individual's educational or retirement expenses that may escalate in cost due to a general increase in price levels.

---

[3] Lehman Brothers is also including IPBs as part of its Treasury, and therefore aggregated, indices. Other index providers, for example, Salomon Brothers, have tended toward distinguishing IPBs as a separate type of investment, and therefore not part of generic bond indexes.

For such investors, long-term IPBs represent the riskless asset. Treasury bills and other money market instruments provide no such assurance of outperforming inflation and in the past have exhibited substantial variability in realized real returns. In addition, few would find a 1% real return (the average long-term historical real return on Treasury bills) strategically compelling. Traditional bonds, which provide a guaranteed nominal return, are quite risky in real terms. Historically, stocks have not been a good hedge against the ravages of inflation, even though they represent financial claims on real assets. Real estate, while a better inflation hedge than equities, is relatively illiquid and impractical for many investors.

One way to generate real returns is to purchase assets that are expected to generate superior nominal performance. In this way, over time, one would expect to outperform inflation during average or even moderately high inflation. However two key issues must first be addressed. First, one must be sure that the nominal performance is truly superior. For example, if IPBs could be purchased with a 3.5% real coupon, and inflation was expected to stay at 3%, holding a riskier 10-year Treasury yielding a 6.5% nominal coupon would be difficult to justify. Second, one must recognize that average returns alone rarely define appropriateness in a strategic context. Depending on the type of institutional investor, varying degrees of attention need to be given to risk management. The implicit and explicit costs associated with a shortfall of a given size generally outweigh the benefits associated with exceeding expectations by the same amount. This is particularly true in a fiduciary context.

Tactical Investors

Some investors opportunistically invest in IPBs. Such tactical investors have overcome the common misgivings regarding IPBs. But the misgivings in the current environment are worth acknowledging.

First, the secular outlook for inflation remains benign, and nominal bonds are already pricing in a substantial expected inflation. Therefore there is a risk that IPBs may underperform traditional bonds. Second, there has been disappointing long-term performance of the U.K. and Canadian IPBs issued in the 1980s and first half of the 1990s. In particular, over this period nominal bonds have handily outperformed IPBs. Third, due to the small market size, unfamiliar risk characteristics, and convenience as a "buy-and-hold" instrument, the broker-dealer community has been reluctant to aggressively devote market-making resources to this asset class. As a result, the liquidity of IPBs has suffered.

Tactical investors in IPBs have addressed these concerns. Even in the context of an outlook for muted inflation, IPBs are appropriate for long-term structural and anticipatory purposes. IPBs have been mediocre performers (in terms of comparative nominal returns) in other countries because they perform best when inflation is increasing, and in the recent past inflation around the globe has plummeted.

With respect to liquidity and market-making in IPBs, their low level of volatility does not tend to attract speculators or market makers, but rather their structure favors long-term investors. This tends to reduce revenues for broker-dealers and results in less liquidity than one might find in traditional *government* bonds. However, traditional government bonds are among the most liquid investments in existence, and set a very high standard. Even at the current stage of development, the IPB market seems to enjoy an equal or greater amount of liquidity than the corporate bond market. For example, institutional investors in Canadian IPBs are routinely afforded the flexibility to trade blocks of C$10 million face value of 30-year IPBs on a bid/ask spread of C$20,000 or less. (In yield terms this bid/ask spread amounts to a mere 0.008%.)

TRADERS AND MARKET MAKERS

The distinction between tactical investors in IPBs and proprietary traders of IPBs is a blurry one. Tactical investors typically have a longer-term perspective and are more focused on identifying re-valuation opportunities that are expected to materialize over a period of weeks, months, or even years. In addition, investors rarely short-sell IPBs. Traders, by contrast, are more focused on identifying specific pockets of supply and demand and concrete opportunities to profit from their insights and market information. Over time horizons of minutes, days, weeks, or months, traders will assume long or short positions in IPBs.

Some traders function as market makers. Market makers focus on profiting from *flow* business. By providing the service of standing by their quoted bids and offers, they are able to charge a bid/ask spread. The higher the volume of flows, the easier it becomes to discern supply and demand trends. This allows them to transact even more aggressively and frequently in terms of size and tightness of the bid/ask spread, which in turn leads to more flows. Ultimately, they profit from the volume of business they transact rather than the direction of market movements.

Section II

Structures and Strategies

Chapter 5

Structure

All the major characteristics of the U.S. Treasury IPBs were announced in September 1996. These characteristics are summarized in Exhibit 1.

The structure of the Treasury IPBs is modeled on the Canadian Real Return Bonds. Basically, inflation protection is provided by indexing the principal amount to the *non-seasonally adjusted* U.S. City Average All Items Consumer Price Index for All Urban Consumers (CPI-U).[1] Having indexed the principal, each semiannual coupon is simply a fixed percentage of the inflation-adjusted principal.

Unfortunately, some of the simplicity of this elegant structure is lost in its implementation, mainly due to operational and technical reasons. In particular, the adjusted-principal value of the bond is more precisely defined in terms of an index ratio. A different index ratio applies to each settlement date. The index ratio is the reference CPI for the settlement date divided by the reference CPI for the issue date. The reference CPI, in turn, differs from the CPI-U in that it is lagged, and its frequency is daily. These differences are necessary for a number of reasons. First, CPI-U for a particular month is reported after the month. A 15-day period is required to tabulate the relevant survey prices and report the results. Second, in order to facilitate settlement on any date between coupon dates, conventions to calculate accrued interest and accrued inflation compensation are needed. A lag of three months is sufficient to facilitate the actual mechanics, including a small buffer to cover contingencies.

An example is instructive. The reference CPI number used for May 1 will be the CPI-U reported for February, which is typically

---

[1] The "headline" inflation figure reported is typically the same series, *seasonally adjusted*. In addition, core CPI, which subtracts the volatile food and energy components, is also widely followed.

Exhibit 1: Terms of US Treasury IPB

Issuer	United States Treasury
Maturity	10-Year Notes and semi-annual Strips. Other maturities, and formats, to be added by 1998
Index	Consumer Price Index (CPI-U)
Real Yield	Determined by competitive auction to be 3.449%; Range of 3.0% to 4.0% expected over first year.
Reference CPI	The reference CPI for the first day of any calendar month is the CPI-U for the third preceding calendar month. The reference CPI for any other day of the month is calculated by a linear interpolation between the reference CPI applicable to the first day of the month and the reference CPI applicable to the first day of the following month
Index Ratio	Reference CPI applicable to a particular settlement date divided by the reference CPI applicable to the original issue date
Principal	Indexed to CPI-U by multiplying the value of principal at issuance by the index ratio applicable to the settlement date.
Minimum Guarantee	Bonds are redeemed at their inflation-adjusted principal, or their par amount, whichever is greater.
Coupon	Semiannual interest is determined by multiplying the inflation-adjusted principal amount by one-half the quoted coupon on each interest payment date
Auction Style	Uniform price ("Dutch") style. Participants will bid a real yield.
Schedule	Auctioned January, April, July, October.
Minimum Size	As with other couponed Treasury instruments, the minimum and incremental denomination to bid, hold or transfer is $1000.00 original principal.
Book-Entry	Maintained and transferred at their original par amount through either the commercial book entry system (TRADES) or TREASURY DIRECT

released around March 15. Daily reference CPI values for other days in May can easily be determined by linear interpolation between the reference CPI values for May 1 and June 1. Consequently, the reference CPI for May 15 is a linear interpolation between February and March CPI-U values.[2] As is the case with all semiannually paying bonds, the coupon payment received is the product of one half of the stated annual coupon rate and the full (inflation adjusted) principal amount.

STRIPS

IPBs are eligible for the STRIPS (Separate Trading of Registered Interest and Principal of Securities) program. This allows principal and interest components to be separated in order to create a series of inflation-protected zero-coupon Treasury securities. Each individual inflation-protected zero is itself inflation protected. The price for each individual "zero" determines a point on the real spot yield curve. Although there can be considerable irregularities in the real spot yield curve, as a whole the spot yield curve must be consistent with the arbitrage bands created by the stripping and reconstitution process of the intact Treasury IPBs.

MINIMUM GUARANTEE

While the recent economic environment has been characterized by inflation, albeit of a subdued, disinflationary nature, questions naturally arise regarding how IPBs would behave during a fall in the general price level, or deflation. In such an instance, the new adjusted-principal value is less than the prior adjusted principal value and this impacts semiannual interest payments accordingly. In other words, interest payments can fall from previous levels. In addition, it is possible for interest payments to be based on adjusted-principal values less than the original principal amount. The Treasury has, however, guaranteed that for the maturity payment itself (and only the maturity payment) the

---

[2] Mathematically the reference CPI interpolation formula is expressed as follows:

$$\text{RefCPI}_{\text{May 15}} = \text{CPI}_{\text{Feb}} + (14/31)(\text{CPI}_{\text{March}} - \text{CPI}_{\text{Feb}})$$

investor cannot receive less than the original principal amount. While some advisors questioned the efficiency of providing such a guarantee, the Treasury decided that the regulatory, institutional, and psychological benefits of providing the guarantee would facilitate distribution of the bonds to an extent that would more than justify the theoretical and contingent cost to the government. From an investor's point of view this is clearly an advantage since the government is freeing the investor from the downward adjustments to principal which would characterize most other inflation hedges in a deflationary environment.

TAXATION POLICY

Prior to the issuance of U.S. Treasury IPBs in January 1997, the government had to determine how inflation compensation would be taxed. Exempting or deferring taxes on inflation compensation would make IPBs more attractive and would lower financing costs on one hand, but would reduce tax receipts on the other.

Regardless of the taxation policy chosen, certain constituencies would benefit to the detriment of others. Ultimately the government decided to tax the securities as much like traditional bonds as possible. So, like zero-coupon bonds, IPBs incur a tax liability on phantom income. Phantom income is income earned but not paid.

This does not mean that investors pay more taxes or that they pay taxes sooner with IPBs than with traditional bonds. For example, if inflation, nominal yields, and tax rates are constant, the cash flow profile of taxes paid and payments received on an IPB is comparable to the profile of taxes paid and payments received on a nominal bond assuming reinvestment of the excess coupon. A negative inflation accrual, which would occur in a year which experienced deflation, would create negative phantom income that could be used to offset other income, with certain limitations. Upon sale, capital gains or losses are realized in the same manner as nominal bonds, except that investors are given full credit, in terms of cost basis, for previously taxed inflation accruals. Conceptually this is no more complicated than the taxation of equity dividends when an automatic dividend reinvestment program is being utilized.

Some 15 years earlier, in 1981, the United Kingdom faced the same question regarding taxation of inflation accruals and selected an equally equitable, but quite different solution. The U.K. tax law was changed to exempt not only the inflation accrual on indexed bonds from taxation, but also capital gains on any long-term asset. In April 1996, the United Kingdom made substantial changes in the tax law which continued to preserve the equitable treatment of disparate asset types. These changes did, however, institute taxes on long-term capital gains that were in excess of inflation on both IPBs and other assets.

THE CONSUMER PRICE INDEX

The BLS methodology for calculation of the CPI is not static. Rather, over time it adapts to changes in consumer behavior and incorporates new developments in our understanding of economics. These changes are undertaken by the BLS with the goal of better measuring the cost of living. Most such changes are "technical" in nature and have a marginal impact on the index as a whole or sub-index components. However, investors in IPBs must assume the risk that these technical changes may alter the CPI in a manner adverse to their interests. (See "Boskin Commission Report" below.)

According to the Uniform Offering Circular, the investor need not assume the risk of the CPI being discontinued, fundamentally altered, or altered by legislation or Executive Order.[3] Adverse changes of these types will cause the Treasury to "substitute an appropriate alternate index." The paragraph in the Circular concludes with the sentence: "Determinations of the Secretary in this regard will be final."

Boskin Commission Report
Dissection of CPI methodology is currently being conducted both inside and outside of Washington. In early December 1996 the Advisory Commission to Study the Consumer Price Index (the Boskin Commission) released its final report to the Senate Finance Committee. The report is entitled "Toward a More Accurate Measure of the Cost of Living." It estimated the upward bias in current CPI as having a plausible

---

[3] Federal Register, January 6, 1997.

range of 0.80 to 1.60 percentage points per annum. The report also included recommendations relating to measuring the cost of living.

Although it is impossible to eliminate all of the concern surrounding how the Boskin report will ultimately impact policy, the Treasury and BLS reduced much of the uncertainty prior to the first auction of IPBs, by responding to the commission's report within a month of its release.

Treasury Response

The Treasury, for the purpose of illustration, first focused on the Commission's recommendation aimed at improving the calculation of the monthly CPI.[4] In the preamble to the amended Uniform Offering Circular, the Treasury stated that such alterations to the calculations of monthly CPI would be considered technical. Such changes could, therefore, impact the nominal yield earned by IPB investors.

However the recommendation relating to the monthly CPI was just a small part of the Commission report. Another suggestion was the construction of a supplementary measure of the cost of living (COL Index) which would introduce improvements in cost of living measurement arising from new information and new research results. Due to more extensive reliance on less timely data inputs, such as consumer expenditure data, the Commission recommended that this series be reported annually.

Subsequently in the preamble to the amended Uniform Offering Circular, the Treasury focused on the Commission's recommendation to create an annual Cost of Living Index. Although not advocated by the Boskin commission, a decision by the BLS to *replace* rather than *supplement* the monthly CPI with such an index would constitute a fundamental change to the CPI. Such a change would therefore precipitate the implementation of an alternate index by the Treasury.

While the Boskin Commission report does carry substantial political and academic weight, it does not set policy or dictate BLS methodology. It also does not represent the only perspective on measuring cost of living. In particular, the BLS has presented a somewhat different perspective.

---

[4] Federal Register, January 6, 1997.

BLS Reaction

After the release of the report, the BLS was quick to point out that the issues identified in the report were not new problems, that in some cases the Commission's estimates were drawn from BLS research, and that the BLS Handbook of Methods guides the operational decision about how to incorporate research results into construction of the CPI. It also pointed out that just as there are imperfections in CPI methodology that cause the CPI to overstate increases in the cost of living, there are other imperfections that cause it to understate increases in the cost of living. Lastly, it highlighted that nearly two-thirds of the Commission's estimated bias in the CPI were based on "alleged deficiencies" in the BLS's treatment of quality changes and new product introductions. The BLS pointed out that hard empirical evidence regarding such issues is extremely limited, that the Commission's estimates of these biases rely heavily on the members' best judgment, and in the words of one Commission member are admittedly "squishy."

In summary, it would be irresponsible for an IPB investor to dismiss the Boskin Commission report as irrelevant. On the other hand, it would be equally irresponsible for investors to conclude that the subjectivity inherent in measuring the CPI precludes investing in IPBs, or that the Boskin Commission recommendations will be summarily adopted.

Chapter 6

Policy Issues

Issuing debt is a key component of a nation's fiscal policy equation. It also indirectly impacts a nation's monetary conditions. In this chapter we focus on the economic policy issues relating to IPB issuance.

WELFARE GAIN OF ISSUING IPBS

IPBs reduce the expected cost of financing a government's total debt because they are free of the inflation risk premium which is built into nominal long-term bond yields. This improves taxpayer welfare by some fraction of the 0.5% to 1.0% inflation risk premium believed to be embedded in nominal bond yields. Investors are not harmed by these lower yields. At the margin they would be indifferent between accepting lower yields versus living with the higher risk of nominal debt. The elimination of this inflation risk premium is a true welfare gain and not simply a transfer of welfare from bond investors to the government. The interest savings is a direct result of the risk reduction that IPBs produce.

EFFICIENT RISK SHARING

Investors have an inherent preference for lower risk assets and assets which meet a particular profile unique to their investment needs. IPBs create a way to offer real risk-free bonds to satisfy these desires. The market will price the IPBs so that they provide expected returns commensurate with their reduced risk level, and allocate them to those investors who have the strongest preference for them. In this way, the market is able to efficiently allocate these lower risk assets, leaving the higher risk assets for those better situated to absorb risk. Individually and in aggregate this reallocation of risk increases welfare.

Existence of a large IPB market might also spur other long-term vehicles denominated in real terms. Areas such as mortgage and insurance products are being explored. This would again allow the marketplace to more effectively price and share risk between participants over specific time periods.

ENHANCEMENT OF MONETARY POLICY CREDIBILITY

Investors demand an inflation risk premium in part because governments have an incentive to devalue the fixed nominal claims against them. This is particularly true in today's environment where political constituencies fight for fewer and fewer discretionary budget dollars. Inflation is an insidious tool of taxation which can be passed by fiat as opposed to other taxes which require the approval of the legislative process. Because investors are not naive to these motivations, they demand compensation for this risk.

A government which can credibly demonstrate that it has reduced or eliminated the flexibility to impose this inflation tax will ultimately, if not immediately, lower its interest costs. Issuance of IPBs reduces the incentive to inflate, because higher inflation compensation on IPBs in an inflationary environment would absorb the additional net governmental revenues created by the increase in inflation. In short, issuance of IPBs makes the foreswearing of the inflation tax more credible. This greater creditability impacts yields on the full rolling stock of nominal debt, which for the U.S. Treasury amounts to more than $5 trillion.

Some critics of IPBs have publicly argued that their issuance reduces the resolve of the most vocal inflation fighting constituencies. This is true. IPBs provide safe harbor for those segments of society most vulnerable to the impacts of inflation, such as retired people living on modest fixed incomes. But any reduction in this anti-inflation political constituency is likely balanced by a reduction in a government's incentive to inflate. The empirical evidence supports those who argue that IPBs reduce inflationary pressures.[1]

---

[1] For example, studies such as M. Persson, T. Persson, and L. Svensson, "Time Consistency of Fiscal and Policy," *Econometrica* (1988) and G. Calvo and P. Guidotti, "Indexation and Maturity of Government Bonds: An Exploratory Model," *Public Debt Management: Theory and History* (1990) conclude that a portion of a government's debt should be indexed.

Moral Hazard[2]

The government is both the issuer of IPBs (Department of Treasury) and publisher of the CPI (BLS, Department of Labor.) Of all the public and private inflation indices considered, the CPI was ultimately selected as the most appropriate for the indexation of IPBs. It is simple, widely followed, timely, and generally representative of inflationary phenomena. Under normal circumstances, the non-seasonally adjusted CPI is not subject to retroactive revisions.

The inherent ambiguity in measuring the CPI (see Consumer Price Index Sub-Section) creates a moral hazard because the government could directly control the economic value of its liability. Fortunately, several factors mitigate against the risk of the government publishing statistics which are not scientifically based.

First, professional integrity and a strong institutional infrastructure largely preclude the government from acting on such opportunities. Second, any confiscation of value through index distortions would be perceived by the financial community as tantamount to default. Since the issuance process is a repeated game[3] of substantial proportion even by government standards, such a "default" would have repercussions on future debt issuance and other governmental promises that would greatly outweigh any apparent economic or political benefits derived. Third, influential political constituencies, such as the retired population, have vested interests in making sure that reported CPI does not understate inflation. These interests go far beyond the direct impact of CPI on their indexed social security benefits. The constituencies with such vested interests will continue to exist, and are in fact growing. And lastly, far greater moral hazards exist in other areas of government, including monetary, fiscal, and social policy, particularly as they impact the real value of the more than $5 trillion in Treasury debt outstanding.

---

[2] "Moral hazard" is a reference to insurance literature. Moral hazard originally referred to the hazard insurance lines in which the insured could directly influence his risk ranking by changing his behavior. For example, an individual who obtains vandalism insurance might become less vigilant about parking his car in a secured space.

[3] "Repeated game" is a reference to game-theory literature. In single round, or non-repeated games, the theory suggests actors will behave opportunistically. In repeated games actors must consider benefits of maintaining a reputation or symbiotic relationships.

TRANSFER OF MARKET INFORMATION

The yield on an IPB along with the yield on a nominal bond of the same maturity can be used to determine the level of future inflation implied by the market.[4] For example, if the differences between yields of nominal bonds and IPBs is higher than current inflation, the market is suggesting that inflation levels, or risks, will increase over time. If the yield differential is lower than current inflation, the market is suggesting that substantial progress will be made toward reducing inflation. Extending this to a full term structure of market yields allows one to determine the implied trajectory of inflation. In particular, given prices for real and nominal STRIPS over a full range of maturities, the market can render implied inflation forecasts over not only specific time horizons (e.g., 10 years) but also for specific years. To the extent that markets are relatively efficient, the implied inflation rate so derived constitutes one of the best available forecasts of inflation and inflation risks. This can serve as an observable measure of a government's inflation fighting credentials.

---

[4] The term "implied" used in this context, by definition, simply means the difference between the two yields, and as such is devoid of any economic content. However, arbitrage pricing theory intimately ties such a difference to risk-neutral expectations of inflation rates. The authors, subsequently, gingerly use the phrase "the market is suggesting." For a more detailed discussion, see the seminal work on the topic of expectations and markets by M. Harrison and D. Kreps, "Martingales and Multiperiod Securities Markets," *Journal of Economic Theory* (1979), pp. 381-408.

Chapter 7

Valuation Methods

Although Treasury IPBs are indexed to inflation and have the full faith and credit of the U.S. Treasury backing them, they are not immune from market induced fluctuations in their value. While generally less volatile than nominal bonds with a similar maturity profile, these securities still require careful analysis. An understanding of the determinants of real interest rates (described in Chapter 3) combined with the basic analytical concepts used to value a floating-rate security form the foundation of IPB valuation.

OVERVIEW

Just as traditional bonds experience fluctuations in market value as a result of changing *nominal* yields, inflation indexed bonds experience fluctuations as a result of changing *real* yields. The mathematics is essentially identical. For example, a 1% increase in market yields on nominal bonds from 6% to 7% will cause just over a 7% drop in the price of a traditional 10-year Treasury. Similarly, a 1% increase in real market yields of IPBs from 3.5% to 4.5% would cause about an 8% drop in the price of a 10-year IPB. In both cases, the bond's price drops in line with its formulaic duration characteristics. IPBs have a higher formulaic duration than conventional bonds because the yields and stated coupon payments are much lower. Just as with nominal bonds, lower discounting rates and lower coupon-cash flows result in a longer present value weighted average term of the cash flows.

This does not mean that IPBs are riskier or have more volatile price movements as a result of higher formulaic durations. In fact, volatilities for similar maturities (or durations) tend to be lower because IPBs only react to the real component of interest rates. Real rates traditionally exhibit much less volatility than nominal yields given that nominal yields respond to both changes in real rates and changes in inflation expectations.

COMPARISONS OF NOMINAL BONDS AND IPBS

The impact that IPBs have as an inflation hedge can be seen when examining the nominal returns of conventional 10-year bonds and IPBs, juxtaposed to the real returns of conventional 10-year bonds and IPBs.

Exhibit 1 highlights a fundamental point. It relates to the definition of a nominal bond and an IPB. A nominal bond promises fixed nominal cash flows, and therefore, a fixed nominal return regardless of inflation rate. An IPB promises fixed real cash flows, and therefore a fixed real return regardless of the inflation rate.[1]

Exhibit 1: Holding Period Returns: Nominal Treasuries versus IPBs Under Different Inflation Scenarios

Inflation Rate over Life of Note	Nominal Return: Traditional Bond	Nominal Return: Inflation-Protection Bond	Real Return: Traditional Bond	Real Return: Inflation Protection Bond
6%	6.5%	9.7%	0.5%	3.5%
5%	6.5%	8.7%	1.4%	3.5%
4%	6.5%	7.6%	2.4%	3.5%
3%	6.5%	6.6%	3.4%	3.5%
2%	6.5%	5.6%	4.4%	3.5%
1%	6.5%	4.5%	5.4%	3.5%
0%	6.5%	3.5%	6.5%	3.5%
−1%	6.5%	2.5%	7.6%	3.5%
−2%	6.5%	1.4%	8.7%	3.5%

[1] If the inflation experiences a dramatic increase, real return can be impacted at the margin. For example, if a 10-year IPB were purchased in a 3% inflation environment and, prior to maturity the inflation rate increased to 15%, the realized real return would be reduced from 3.00% per annum to about 2.88%. This is a result of indexation lag, which for U.S. IPB is quoted as 3 months, but actually has an average day delay from the announcement of an inflation report of 30 days.

HISTORICAL DETERMINANTS OF REAL INTEREST RATES

The magnitude of fluctuations in market values of IPBs is a function of the volatility of real interest rates. While less volatile than nominal interest rates, real rates in the United Kingdom and other economies where they are directly observable, do fluctuate. Investors in IPBs need to carefully consider the current macroeconomic environment and its implications for real interest rates.

As discussed in Chapter 6, real interest rates can be thought of as the price of funds determined by the interaction between those who supply capital (savers) and those who demand capital (borrowers). The global supply of investable capital is identically determined by global savings rates. Savings can come from three areas: individuals, corporations, and public entities. Demand for capital is largely determined by the level of real investment. This includes investment abroad as well as domestically because demand in one region spills over directly and indirectly to create demand on the world's total pool of capital. Analysis of the forces impacting savings rates and investment demand lies at the heart of formulating an outlook for real interest rates.

Supply of Capital

The global supply of investment capital is equal to the aggregate national savings rates. Analysis performed by the International Monetary Fund (IMF) breaks the history of world savings rates over the past three and a half decades into three distinct periods: the *pre-oil shock years*, 1960-1972; the *years of adjustment to the oil shock*, 1973-1980; and the *post-oil shock period*, 1981 to 1994. (See Exhibit 2.) Savings rates have clearly fallen in the most recent period, averaging only 22.5% of GDP versus more than 25% in the oil shock period. A closer look at the savings data reveals that private savings have remained virtually unchanged while public savings have fallen from an average of 4% of GDP in the 1960-72 period to near 0.5% today. This decline in global public savings can most directly be attributed to an increase in fiscal deficits in the major industrialized nations.[2]

---

[2] IMF, "Savings in a Growing World Economy," *World Economic Outlook* (1995).

Exhibit 2: Secular Trends in Global Savings Rates
World Savings Rate

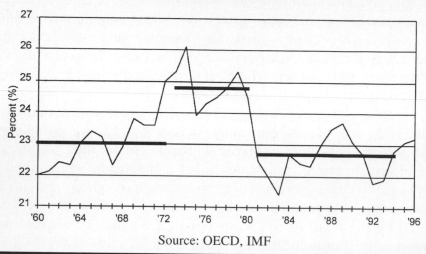

Source: OECD, IMF

In contrast, the developing nations have seen savings rates rise from 19% in 1970 to 27% in 1994. This was largely due to the 13% rise in savings rates in Asia. These nations also experienced extraordinarily high rates of GDP growth over the same time period. This naturally raises the question: does savings create growth or does growth create more savings? There is a good deal of evidence that the causality runs in both directions and, with some luck, builds on itself, forming a virtuous circle.[3] This is important as international capital markets are forced to consider the impact of financing Asia's rather substantial development needs. The body of recent analysis tends to support the view that higher growth rates will also result in higher savings rates that will allow these nations to largely self-finance their continued development, and thus not unduly strain the world's supply of savings.

Fiscal Policy

Excessive government borrowing impacts real interest rates since higher deficits are a direct call on a nation's, and the world's, supply of savings. Increased government demand for capital puts upward

---

[3] In contrast, we fear that the causality between low savings and low growth may build upon itself, forming a vicious cycle in many of the developed nations.

pressure on interest rates as supply and demand determine an equilibrium. This is the classic explanation of how deficits impact interest rates and crowd out private investment.

A change in government policies, however, may well already be underway. Europe's scramble to satisfy Maastrict[4] criteria, the precipitous decline in U.S. budget deficits from almost $300 billion per year in 1992 to barely $100 billion in 1996, and Japan's recognition that its financial strength is far from unlimited, suggest that the tidal wave of government deficits characterizing much of the 1980s and early 1990s may now be subsiding. In fact, some countries, such as New Zealand, are already running budget surpluses and paying down debt. Countries that are reducing deficits, and those which are running surpluses, are presumably freeing up capital for private sector deployment and reducing upward pressure on global real rates.

Demand for Capital

As discussed above, emerging economies largely fund investment through internal savings, and so their rapid development may not have a major impact on the net demand for capital worldwide. However, perceptions that the returns on investments are increasing (whether such perceptions are precipitated out of rising corporate profitability or identification of opportunities for development of public infrastructure) generally create demand for capital. For example, recent high levels of corporate earnings have caused increased investment in plant and equipment. The higher rates of expected return on investments can thereby lead to higher interest rates.

The period covered by the most recent bull market (1980-1996) in equities is highlighted in Exhibit 3. Rates of return on equity capital fell until 1982 and then began to rise. The fact that equity prices rose consistently during the second half of this period supports the argument that profitable investment opportunities were being identified, and that these opportunities were increasing the demand for capital. In line with the model described above, this would help explain the rise in G-10 real interest rates over the same period.[5]

---

[4] "Maastrict criteria" refers to the dimensions upon which entry into the European Monetary Union is to be determined for member countries.

[5] Ifty Islam, *Merrill Spread Focus: Real Interest Rates*, 1996.

Exhibit 3: Rates of Return in the Business Sector

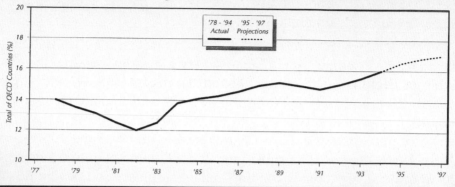

Global Capital Markets

Although students of economic history know that the current wave of globalization is not the first, cross border capital flows measured as a percent of GDP have increased during the last decade to levels not seen since before World War I. This is the result of a number of factors including greatly enhanced information technology resources, a reduction in governmental controls by both host and investor countries, and a broader acceptance of modern portfolio theory and its implications for portfolio diversification. Structural changes in the world economy, namely the entrance of a host of developing nations which had previously followed more inwardly focused development strategies, have increased the number of potentially attractive investment opportunities as well. The impact can be seen in the capital flows data for the OECD countries shown in Exhibit 4.

Net capital flows have increased two or three times from the early 1980s to the mid 1990s. Other measures of the impact of international investors are reflected in the Bank of International Settlements (BIS) data which indicate that by the second half of 1993 total international securities transactions for the G-7 countries amounted to over $6 trillion and that 20-25% of all government bonds were held by non-residents.[6] Together these data clearly offer the scope for international participants, as the marginal investors, to exert substantial influence on markets, thus helping to create more uniform real interest rates across national boundaries. A recent study by the IMF

---

[6] *Bank for International Settlements Annual Report* (1994).

lends support for this argument when it revealed that global fiscal variables were far more statistically significant than national fiscal variables in the determination of real rates for specific countries.[7]

Exhibit 4: Macroeconomic Determinants of Real Yields: Major Capital Flows in Selected Industrial Countries[1]

	1976-80	1981-85	1986-90	1991	1992	1993	1994
	in billions of US dollars, annual averages						
	Total capital flows						
Outflows[2]	153.7	231.1	678.9	510.8	543.6	975.7	725.8
As a percentage of GDP	3.0	2.9	5.4	3.3	3.2	5.3	3.6
United States	43.3	44.1	77.4	96.9	82.5	125.4	164.3
Japan	15.4	53.5	242.2	117.2	25.4	65.0	162.0
Western Europe[4]	95.0	133.5	359.2	296.7	435.7	785.3	399.5
Inflows	168.2	270.7	745.6	510.4	557.6	941.8	635.7
As a percentage of GDP	3.3	3.4	5.9	3.3	3.3	5.1	3.2
United States	33.6	100.0	177.7	82.1	108.2	160.7	278.2
Japan	15.2	30.3	178.3	27.2	-93.5	-43.0	30.8
Western Europe[4]	119.4	140.4	389.6	401.1	542.9	824.1	326.6
	of which: Portfolio investment						
Outflows[2]	21.3	63.6	182.7	267.3	244.1	424.6	232.6
United States	5.3	6.5	13.6	44.7	45.1	120.0	60.6
Japan	3.4	25.0	85.9	74.3	34.4	51.7	83.6
Western Europe[4]	12.6	32.0	83.1	148.3	164.6	253.0	88.4
Inflows	26.3	68.3	172.3	354.0	305.8	520.4	175.4
United States	5.2	29.4	44.7	54.0	66.7	104.9	91.5
Japan	5.1	12.6	26.9	115.3	8.2	-11.1	34.7
Western Europe[4]	16.1	26.4	100.7	184.8	230.9	426.5	49.3
	of which: Direct investment						
Outflows[2]	36.9	37.0	149.4	169.8	157.8	160.5	186.4
United States	16.9	7.6	25.3	31.3	41.0	57.9	58.4
Japan	2.3	5.1	32.1	30.7	17.2	13.7	17.9
Western Europe[4]	17.8	24.3	92.0	107.8	99.6	88.9	110.0
Inflows	23.3	33.2	114.2	101.0	84.8	88.5	123.5
United States	9.0	18.6	53.4	26.1	9.9	21.4	60.1
Japan	0.1	0.3	0.3	1.4	2.7	0.1	0.9
Western Europe[4]	14.2	14.3	60.6	73.6	72.2	67.0	62.5

[1] Excluding official monetary movements.
[2] Including errors and omissions.
[3] Including net short-term capital of the non-bank sector.
[4] Including intra-regional flows.
Data for 1994 are partly estimated.
Sources: IMF, OECD, national data, BIS estimates, and Merrill Lynch

[7] Robert Ford and Douglas Laxton, "World Public Debt and Real Interest Rates," IMF working paper (March 1995).

Country Specific Real Rate Variables and IPBs

While some convergence is expected, real yields will also reflect disparate country specific factors such as market liquidity, the real effective exchange rate,[8] and technical nuances in the structure, taxation, or quotation of their IPBs. Less liquidity seems to require higher real yields, as does investment in those currencies which are overvalued. A 1995 OECD study also pointed to factors such as a country's debt to GDP ratio, government deficit, current account and past inflation history as important in determining real yields.[9]

The major problem with analyzing past nominal yields and comparing them to potential real bond yields on IPBs is identifying which part of a bond's nominal yield is real yield and which is the bond's expected inflation and inflation risk premium. Theoretically, the fiscal and trade issues outlined in the OECD model should bear largely on the bond's risk premium, and thus not significantly affect real interest rates on IPBs. This is because the bond inflation risk premium for a sovereign local currency bond is largely the risk of unexpected inflation. The traditional credit concerns (risk of non-payment) is virtually non-existent, even for second tier countries, because a government can always print sufficient currency to cover any nominal value of outstanding debt. Only its willingness to take this step to avoid default is in question.

Arguments focused on attributing interest rate differentials to secular currency trends are also less applicable to IPBs than to nominal bonds. If the expected depreciation of a currency is mainly ascribed to inflation differentials between the two countries, then the IPBs would be largely insulated. A further discussion of IPBs and currency is provided later when we discuss foreign currency exposure management.

Markets in Other Countries and U.S. Real Rates

Past performance of IPBs in other countries is also of limited use in analyzing fair value for U.S. real yields. This is because of the low

---

[8] Economists, most notably R. Dornbush, have written extensively on the equilibrium dynamics of exchange rates and real effective exchange rates.

[9] Malcolm Edey and Adrlon Orr, "The Determinants of Real Long-Term Interest Rates: 17 Country-Pooled-Time Series Evidence," OECD working papers (1995).

liquidity and the unique domestic investor base in each country. For example, in the United Kingdom where capital gains taxes are indexed and the IPB market is more than six times the size of the next largest IPB market, real yields have been consistently lower than in either Canada, Australia, or Sweden. The United States is also unique because of its status as the world's reserve currency. Other nations' central banks are forced, in effect, to hold dollars in order to both manage their currencies and conduct international trade. Foreign individuals also hold dollars due to their convenience as an international medium of exchange. These natural holders of dollars have allowed the United States to maintain lower than expected nominal yields given its inflation rates and economic profile.

MEASURES OF EXPOSURE

There are various common uses of the term "duration." For nominally oriented fixed income investors the most relevant is generally effective duration. Effective duration is a forward looking estimate of an investment's price sensitivity to a parallel shift in nominal yields. It is calculated as follows:

$$\text{Duration}_{\text{Effective}} = -\frac{\text{Percentage Change in Price}}{\text{Given 1\% Change in Nominal Yields}}$$

The price of a floater is not directly impacted by parallel shifts in yields since the intention is for the floating coupons to reflect prevailing interest rates or changes thereof. In particular, a change in current or future interest rates impacts the income earned to the same extent that they impact the rate at which cash flows are discounted. And so, at *first* cut the effective duration of a floater is zero.

The price of a floater is, however, *indirectly* impacted by nominal yield shifts. For example, if changes in nominal yields are associated with changes in the credit of the issuer, then the price of the floater will exhibit sensitivity to yield shifts and so will exhibit a non-zero effective duration. In addition, if a floater's market price is not near par, as would be the case for a floater issued at par by a company that subsequently experienced significant credit deterioration, price changes would be associated with changes in nominal yields. For most floaters these indirect impacts are small and for many purposes ignored. As such, their durations are typically assumed to be determined by the next reset date.

However, the indirect impact of nominal yield shifts on price may be substantial for IPBs, and should be reflected in any reported effective duration estimates. In particular, because the index which determines income earned, namely the CPI, does not perfectly track nominal yields, changes in nominal yields can be associated with changes in prices.

In practice, estimating effective durations of IPBs is best accomplished in a two-step process. The first step is mechanical and involves determining the real duration (defined below) of the IPB. The difficult and subjective second step is one in which the analyst quantifies the relationship between nominal and real interest rates. This quantification should, at a minimum, incorporate historical, forward-looking, structural, and market-based concepts.

Real Duration

Real duration is a measure of the expected life of a inflation-protection investment. In particular, it incorporates the real size and timing of payments on a real discounted present value basis. Real durations often reflect the long maturity common among inflation-protection securities. A high real duration, or long maturity, of an inflation-protection security is associated with a low expected price volatility when compared to the expected volatility of a nominal bond with a similar *nominal duration* or maturity. This is because real interest rates are generally less volatile than nominal interest rates. An inflation-protection security with a 10-year maturity and a 3.5% real yield would have a real duration of about 8.5 years.

Relationship between Nominal and Real Yields

Simple empirical analysis of market data may lead to grossly misstated effective durations. In particular, over small ranges of yield changes, as characterize the recent history of IPBs, real interest rates seem to exhibit positive correlation with nominal yields. However, a bigger picture perspective questions how real yields would be related to nominal yields if nominal yields were to change dramatically. Specifically, what would happen in a dramatic sell-off of the long-dated fixed income market.

This question is more easily answered if one considers the 1970s. The sell-off in the fixed income market, which led to 10-year nominal bond yields exceeding 15% at their peak later in 1981, was driven by accelerating inflation. In such an environment *ex post*, realized, real yields on nominal bonds of all maturities were negative. Not surprisingly, surveys of market participants indicated that the demand for IPBs, bonds which were unavailable but could insulate against further ravages of inflation, was extremely strong. Some indicated that there were even large investors that would have locked in negative real yields for long periods of time, just to obtain contractual inflation protection. It is difficult to imagine how, or why, market participants would respond to accelerating inflation any differently in the future.

If accelerating inflation, and dramatically higher bond yields are associated with negative, or even just lower, real yields on IPBs, then the effective duration of IPBs is in fact negative.

Modified Real Duration
Modified real duration is closely related to real duration and is a measure of the percentage price change of an inflation-protection security associated with a given change in real interest rates. An inflation-protection security with a 10-year maturity and a 3.5% real coupon would have a modified real duration of about 8.4 years if real yields were 3.5%. Frequently the terms "real duration" and "modified real duration" are used interchangeably, even though technically there are slight differences.

Application of Modified Real Duration
As discussed above, real durations are useful in calculating effective durations. They are also useful in and of themselves. It is the substantial real durations of IPBs that result in the potential for relatively high levels of volatility to be exhibited by IPBs. Even though this high real duration does not imply a high effective duration (because real yields are only partially related to nominal interest rates), high real durations are a measure of how sensitive these bonds can be to arbitrary changes in real yields.

This is the same principal that creates some volatility in the price of floating-rate securities. With floating-rate securities, it is important to carefully analyze the spread duration. A security with a very low index duration and effective duration can exhibit significant price volatility if its spread or real duration is large.

IMPACT OF ISSUER CREDIT ON QUOTED REAL YIELDS

The market's assessment of the credit quality of a corporate IPB issuer is asserted in the difference between the real yield offered by the issue and the real yield of the Treasury IPB benchmark. This difference is generally called the "spread." However, care must be taken to adjust for structural differences, such as different final maturities or reference indices, between the two instruments to ensure that an "apples to apples" comparison is being made.

A positive initial spread over the Treasury bond is usually necessary to compensate the investor primarily for the default risk of corporate IPBs. Subsequent deterioration or improvement of credit quality is expressed through a widening or narrowing of the spread.

The spread does not have to be positive. If the bond has qualities that make it preferable to Treasuries, then its spread will be negative, and it will trade with a lower real yield than Treasuries. This would be unusual, and would suggest that bond were a municipal bond (with tax advantages), a putable bond (with embedded options), or a bond that had some other inherent structural features.

Chapter 8

IPBs Around the Globe

Currently, numerous countries have IPBs outstanding, and several are worth mentioning. The U.K. market is large and extremely liquid. In addition, Canada, Australia, and New Zealand have issued in large enough quantities to ensure reasonable liquidity. While each of these markets shares the basic inflation protection concept with their newly issued U.S. cousins, there are some differences worth noting. Some of these are market size, trading liquidity, time lag associated with the inflation indexation, taxation, and day-count and quotation conventions. These differences can create substantial impacts on both observed quoted real yields and "true" real yield available to investors.

UNITED KINGDOM

The United Kingdom was the first to develop a substantial market for IPBs. With over U.S. $77 billion[1] of IPBs currently outstanding, it has by far the largest and most liquid IPB market. The United Kingdom has also benefited by issuing an entire yield curve of maturities which has helped establish relative valuation along the real yield curve as in the nominal bond market. The principal demand for IPBs in the United Kingdom has come from domestic insurance companies and pension plans which hold slightly more than two-thirds of the outstanding value.

The primary technical difference with the U.S. Treasury structure is that in the United Kingdom both interest and principal are based off of the price index eight months prior to receipt. This lag of eight months was instituted to ensure that the next receivable coupon could be determined in advance of the period to which it relates, simplifying the calculation of settlement date accrued income. The time lag becomes especially detrimental in a rapidly accelerating inflation

---

[1] Quantities expressed in terms of market values outstanding on 12/31/96.

environment, something we have not experienced in the last 15 years. The inflation index reference in the United Kingdom is termed the "Retail Price Index," or simply the RPI.

CANADA

Canadian IPBs were first issued on December 10, 1991. A negative inflation report occurred immediately following the introduction, resulting in a downward adjustment of principal value. This would be only the first in a series of setbacks that stymied the development of this market. As a result this market grew slowly, and remains small compared to the U.K. market. Based on this slow development, the Canadian government delayed issuing a second maturity until December 1995 and so as of January 1997 only two issues, totaling U.S. $5.25 billion, are outstanding. With maturities in 2021 and 2026, the market does not enjoy the benefit of a full yield curve.

From a structural perspective, Canadian IPBs are virtually identical to their U.S. Treasury counterparts. In fact, the Canadian bonds were used as a structural model for U.S. Treasury IPBs.

AUSTRALIA

In contrast to the United Kingdom, Australia's IPB market is much smaller both in absolute value ($3.7 billion for Australia versus $77 billion for the United Kingdom) and as a percentage of total government bonds outstanding (4% versus 20%). Australian issuers also tend to be a more diverse group, with provincial governments and private issuers having contributed to the marketplace in a variety of different structures. The result is a market more complex and fragmented than the United Kingdom, where the vast majority of the issues have been issued by the Bank of England. Australian buyers of IPBs also tend to be a more diverse universe with commercial banks, investment houses, credit unions, building societies, and other fund managers making purchases along with traditional institutional participants such as insurance companies and pension funds.[2]

---

[2] R. McFall Lomm, "U.S. Inflation-Indexed Bonds," *Economics and Risk Focus* (September 6, 1996).

The structure of Australian IPBs is very similar to that of the U.S. Treasury and Canadian IPBs. Principal and interest are calculated using the same basic reference value approach, but CPI is released only on a quarterly basis. As a result, interest payments are based on the average percentage change in CPI over the two quarters ending in the quarter which is two quarters prior to the coupon payment date. For example, a coupon payment in February would be based on CPI for the second and third quarters of the previous year. Depending on the taxation status of an investor, Australian IPBs may be subject to withholding taxes.

INTERNATIONAL RELATIVE VALUE OPPORTUNITIES

The existence of multiple international IPBs offers opportunities not only to express a market view on the level of inflation and real interest rates in countries, but also to express views regarding the relationship of real interest rates across these markets. This presents relative value opportunities as countries' IPBs trade at different real interest rates.

Exhibit 1 highlights relative value relationships on 12/20/96 together with ancilliary data for seven of the large issuers of IPBs. The first two columns, "Hedged Carry" and "Real Yield," report two naive measures of relative value. Hedged Carry is a short-term measure of relative value, and is obtained by subtracting the two-year nominal yield from the implied nominal yield of the IPB. Real Yield is a longer term measure of relative value.

As long as the world continues on its current secular trend in which capital is increasingly able to move across borders to find the best risk-adjusted return, real interest rates should continue to converge. If the bonds are indexed, and therefore changes in inflation rates do not impact valuations, the inflation risk premium should not come into play. In addition, as capital mobility increases, it follows that currencies will not be systematically over- or under-valued. The only differential risk is then the credit of the particular country, which for sovereign issuers in the major industrialized countries is likely to be small. Thus, capital should flow to the country with the highest yielding real return bonds, thereby reducing their yields and reinforcing convergence trends.

Exhibit 1: IPBs Around the Globe Tactical Relative Value Summary

Hedged Carry	Real Yield	Country	Inflation OutLook	Implied Yield	2 Year Comp	Supply (MM)
0.99%	4.23%	Australia (Index Linked: 20 Yrs)	3.0%	7.23%	6.24%	TBA 1H97
1.63%	4.09%	Canada (Real Return Bonds: 30 Yrs)	1.7%	5.79%	4.16%	Qtrly Auction 3/5/9/7: C$ 500
−3.00%	7.00%	Mexico (UDI Bonos: 3 Yrs)	16.0%	23.00%	26.00%	Bi Wkly Auct: NP 150
−0.66%	4.85%	New Zealand (Capital Indexed: 20 Yrs)	1.5%	6.35%	7.01%	Qrtly Auction 2/97
1.23%	4.05%	Sweden (Index Linked Zeros: 5 Yrs)	1.8%	5.85%	4.62%	Taps: Demand Driven
−0.34%	3.43%	UK (Index Linked Gilts: 10 Yrs)	2.9%	6.33%	6.67%	Taps: GBP 300
0.80%	3.50%	US (Inflation-Protection: 10 Yrs)	3.1%	6.60%	5.80%	Nov '96/Early '97 $2,000

Source: The Economist Poll December 1996 and Merrill Lynch December 20, 1996

In practice, the world is still far away from perfectly free capital movements. Even with free capital flows, the stickiness of domestic prices and wages are the subject of perennial academic study. Real interest rates for IPBs will, at least in the near term, be impacted by economic fundamentals such as current account deficits, public sector finances, and deviations from purchasing power parity. What seems clear is that the continuing integration of world capital markets will create opportunities for international investors to express their views regarding the differences between the major IPB markets.

MANAGING FOREIGN CURRENCY EXPOSURE

As is the case for investors in any foreign currency denominated instrument, the investor in foreign IPBs must decide whether to assume exposure to the foreign currency embedded in the instrument, or to hedge the exposure into the home currency. Typically this would be accomplished by offsetting the embedded exposure through a delayed settlement sale of the currency in the forward market. While it is quite clear that the hedging of conventional bonds into the investor's home currency often makes sense, the logic is far less mechanical for IPBs.

Foreign IPBs are "real" assets that expose holders to fluctuations in *real* exchange rates, but insulate, or "protect" holders from fluctuations in exchange rates caused by inflation. In particular, IPBs inherently immunize investors from changes in currency levels, provided that the changes are caused by changes in relative price levels. This immunization is accomplished through the inflation indexation of coupon and principal payments. Empirically (particularly over long time horizons) appreciating currencies are associated with low inflationary regimes and thus low nominal yields, while depreciating currencies are symptomatic of high inflation and thus high nominal yields.

Thus, IPBs expose investors to fluctuations in real exchange rates, but implicitly immunize investors against fluctuations due to inflation. Therefore, naive currency hedging of IPBs, by selling 100% of the foreign currency value forward, would accomplish the goal of hedging the investor against fluctuations in real exchange rates, but would simultaneously "over-hedge" the investor against changes in relative inflation rates. This could actually increase the volatility of returns measured in the domestic currency.

Example: No Foreign-Exchange Hedging in a Classical World

As an example, consider a U.S. investor who buys a Canadian IPB *without* any hedging sales of currency. This investor now has primarily bought exposure to the *real* impact of Canada's monetary and fiscal policies. If Canada decides to embark upon an overly expansionary monetary policy, this laxness, in a classical world with completely flexible exchange rates and capital flows, will be directly translated into the nominal phenomena of a declining currency and an increased inflation rate. The declining currency will clearly hurt the holders of nominal Canadian dollar securities when measured in U.S. dollars. However, for IPB holders currency depreciation would be, in theory, offset by the larger coupon payments and principal accretion associated with inflation.

Conversely, if the Canadian currency were to appreciate as a result of very tight monetary policy, this currency gain would likely be offset by the lower indexed coupon and principal accretion associated with lower inflation. Since the currency movements and indexation effects would largely offset one another, the unhedged investor in IPBs obtains a low risk, real return from both a Canadian perspective and U.S. perspective. In a such a classical framework, the real return obtained is independent of the currency in which it is denominated.

Example: Complete Foreign-Exchange Hedging in a Classical World

In this hypothetical classical world, if the investor were to buy the Canadian IPB *with* hedging of the foreign currency into U.S. dollars, the hedge would profit from a loose policy, depreciating currency environment, just as the IPB was also benefitting from large coupon payments. Tight policy would see the Canadian currency rise versus the U.S. dollar resulting in a loss on the hedge, just as the coupon and principal payments on the IPB were being reduced. Rather than hedging volatility, selling currency in the forward market would amplify the risk of the IPB.

Fluctuations in Real Exchange Rates and Optional Hedging
This suggests that unhedged IPBs seem to make sense in the long run, over which classical economics applies. However, the foreign exchange markets are subject to short-term volatility which is not explained by the classical purchasing power parity logic implicit in the above analysis. In other words, inflation differentials are only one force driving changes in exchange rates, fluctuations in "real exchange" rates are also important. In the case of highly industrialized countries, for which inflation is relatively muted, volatility in real exchange rates account for most of the currency volatility experienced over months, years, and even decades. The implication is that currency movements are often independent of inflation differentials and thus independent of coupon and principal accretion on IPBs.

The hedge which results in the maximum risk reduction will therefore depend on what fraction of the currency volatility is caused by fluctuations in real exchange rates, and what fraction is caused by fluctuations in inflation differentials. The answer will certainly depend on what countries are involved, and what time horizons the investor is targeting.

Section III

Intermediation of IPBs

Chapter 9

Institutional Fund Management

IPBs indirectly purchased through intermediaries offer a variety of opportunities for both institutional and retail investors. The market will continue to evolve rapidly as the investment management community responds with an expanding array of products to take advantage of this evolving asset class.

The "top down" investment process common to most institutional organizations can generally be broken down into three stages. First, distinct asset classes are defined. Next, an allocation to each class is determined. Third, the investment management decisions implementing the given allocation are made.

Forward looking investment committees are already evaluating how they intend to utilize IPBs within this framework. Many view IPBs as a new strategic asset class adding to the existing asset classes of equities, bonds, and cash. Other investment committees are not yet looking at the asset class strategically, but still allow for tactical use of IPBs within other asset classes. One approach we have been advocating, and which is already being employed by some organizations, is to perform all asset allocation analysis in terms of real return rather than nominal return.

A starting point for such an analysis is to list the historical real returns and risks for major asset classes. We have done this in Exhibit 1, including estimated risk and return for IPBs. Such a list is just a starting point, since historical data only provide context.

Since "Real Return" is not currently a broadly used term in finance, a definition is in order. Real (or inflation-adjusted) return is a measure of the increase in purchasing power of an investment. It is equal to the increase in real market value of the investment over the course of a period divided by the real market value of the investment at the beginning of the period. For example, if an investment were to increase in real market value from $1,000 to $1,030 (both market values measured in the purchasing power of one 1987 dollar) the real return would be 3%.

Exhibit 1: Long-Term Real Return and Real Risk for U.S. Asset Classes

Asset[*]	Real Return	Real Risk	Return/Risk
Cash	0.6%	4.2%	0.1
Nominal Bonds	2.1%	7.1%	0.3
Equities	7.2%	20.6%	0.3
IPBs[**]	3.0%	4.2%	0.7

* Ibbotson, 1926 - 1995
** Risk and return data are not available for the U.S. market, these values represent the authors' estimates.

A high real return is not necessarily associated with a high (nominal) total return. For example, in a deflationary environment a high real return could be associated with a low (nominal) total return, or possibly even a loss of (nominal) capital. The 3% real return above could be associated with a 1% (nominal) total return if the purchasing power of a nominal dollar increased by about 2%. Alternately, the 3% real return could be associated with a 13% (nominal) total return if the purchasing power of a nominal dollar fell by about 10%. However, a high real return is always associated with an increase in purchasing power.

STRATEGIC PERFORMANCE BENCHMARK

Once the size of a strategic allocation has been determined, the allocation needs to be implemented and managed. The allocation can either be managed internally, by employees of the sponsoring institution, or externally, by a manager. In either case, performance benchmarks are a critical component of the delegation process.

Currently in the U.S. market only one Treasury IPB exists, so the performance benchmark simply tracks the market value and total return of a portfolio with a 100% investment in the single security. The Lehman Brothers Inflation-Linked Treasury Index does just that. Performance attribution of the benchmark returns dissects the total return of the benchmark into interest income, inflation adjustment, and capital gains. Capital gains can be further broken down, just as capital gains on nominal bonds can be broken down, into accretion of discount, roll-down, and changes in the real yield curve.

Custom inflation protection benchmarks can also be created. They can be based off Inflation Protected STRIPS, mixtures of cash, traditional bonds and IPBs, levered IPBs, or global IPBs.

Investment Latitude

In addition to simply assigning a benchmark, the delegation process includes a clear communication of the degree of investment latitude allowed. The degree of investment latitude is only partially communicated by restrictions on the types and concentrations of securities permitted. Equally important is a qualitative or quantitative indication of how much performance variation from the benchmark is expected. (The excess returns over the benchmark possible are in effect constrained by the limits on risk, or underperformance imposed.)

The most restrictive limits on investment latitude require essentially complete replication of index performance. This approach is termed passive management or indexation. Some oversight is still required to handle, for example, subscriptions, withdrawals, and rebalancing.

The advantage of passive management is that tight tracking of a performance benchmark is assured, and management expenses are minimized. While this approach has its proponents, it is guaranteed to leave any potential value added of active management on the table, and, in essence, to result in below index performance. While this may be acceptable in certain circumstances and for certain sectors, in general it ignores the sources of value added that active management can bring. These sources of value added for traditional bonds are well documented; however, for IPB mandates, the jury is still out. Below the potential sources of value added for IPBs are described in some detail.

SOURCES OF ADDED VALUE

The sources of added valued in the context of IPB mandates are much like those of traditional mandates. Some of these sources thrive on the immaturity of the market, while others will develop only as the market evolves.

Duration
As with conventional bond portfolios, duration management can have a large impact on both absolute and relative performance. IPBs present particular challenges given their long real durations. Duration management of IPB portfolios has the added dimension of requiring investors to manage both real and nominal interest rate risk. Given that performance benchmarks are still in their infancy, bogeys are often customized, which further complicates duration management. On the other hand, it is exactly this immaturity of the market and of approaches to managing IPBs which provide the most attractive opportunities to add value through active management.

International IPBs
Since real interest rates are increasingly determined by the marginal international investor in a global supply and demand framework, a dedicated IPB portfolio should include the discretion to invest in the other IPB markets around the world. This can be especially beneficial given the higher real yields often found outside the U.S. market. While it is true that yield gains from investing can be eroded by the adverse impact of relative real yields diverging, fluctuations in real yields are much lower than fluctuations in nominal yields.

Currency and currency hedging expertise is central to success in managing IPBs globally. Given the complex and unique technical issues associated with hedging IPBs discussed previously, yield differentials cannot be efficiently harvested through naive unhedged, or naive hedged, strategies.

Yield Curve Strategies
Other avenues for value added that professional separate account management often brings to a portfolio include identifying relative value opportunities between different parts of the real yield curve as well as within the conventional coupon curve. Various parts of the real yield curve perform differently, and active management can take advantage of the identified dynamics. The U.S. Treasury IPBs are STRIP eligible 10-year bonds, and therefore can be transformed into a complete series of semiannual zero-coupon IPB maturities from 6 months to 10 years. The Treasury also has plans to issue additional maturities in the future.

Sector Rotation

As the international and U.S. IPB markets evolve, the array of corporate and agency issuers who choose to borrow on a real yield basis will undoubtedly expand. Traditional sector analysis is being extended to include IPBs. This will be especially important as below investment grade companies with real revenue streams begin to issue IPBs. Similarly, relative value no doubt fluctuates between the inflation protection market and the conventional Treasury market.

Conventional instruments, especially of the short-term, cash-equivalent, or floating-rate types, can be seen as another "inflation-protected" sector since their coupons are based on money market yields. Although money market yields do not perfectly track inflation, they do certainly respond, generating higher income in inflationary scenarios and lower income in deflationary scenarios. This simply adds a host of tools to utilize in adding value against inflation-protected benchmarks.

Forward Purchases and cpiPLUS

While currently in their infancy, over-the-counter and exchange-traded forwards, futures, and options markets based on IPBs will evolve. This evolution will increase the opportunity to establish positions and add more value in IPB mandates. In particular, these markets often can provide a cheaper way to obtain exposure to a sector. In other cases IPB derivatives may provide a cheaper way to hedge, or sell, exposure.

IndexPLUS is a management strategy developed by Pacific Investment Management Company (PIMCO) that consistently has allowed investors to outperform passive indexes. IndexPLUS investors obtain complete exposure to an index in a cheap or fairly priced futures market. This leaves almost all cash available for active, "LIBOR PLUS," cash management strategies. This approach has been highly successful in a variety of markets, and is the cornerstone of PIMCO's StocksPLUS equity strategy.

cpiPLUS involves forward purchases of IPBs, which frees up most of the cash value of an investment. Even though the complete market exposure of the IPBs is owned, it is controlled with a small portion of the actual cash outlays. The additional liquidity available allows for cash equivalent investment strategies designed to consistently outperform LIBOR.

Cash strategies that consistently outperform LIBOR are generally characterized by slight extensions of duration, diversified credit risk, and other active, low risk, value added strategies which are identified. While some would consider this leverage, others would not, particularly if the cash raised is kept in cash equivalent securities.

This strategy was first, and most successfully, employed to deliver consistent above average returns to clients in other contexts soon after the development of the financial futures/forward market. It has been found that at the onset of new markets there are often large discrepancies between the cash and derivative markets, creating significant opportunities for sophisticated investors. As the markets become more efficient, there are fewer obvious opportunities, and increasingly sophisticated analysis and tools need to be deployed in order to add significant value relative to cash markets.

INSTITUTIONAL VEHICLES

Separate Account Management

For those large institutional investors who have opted for IPBs as a strategic allocation and desire to take full advantage of the above sources of value added, a dedicated portfolio of these assets managed as a separate account is an attractive means of obtaining this exposure. In addition, such bonds can often be purchased tactically within existing separate account mandates.

Strategic Mandates and Immunization Strategies At this stage, strategic inflation-protected mandates are often loosely structured. The industry has not yet evolved to incorporate the high degree of precision, or standardization, that is characteristic of equity or core bond mandates. Some inflation-protected mandates are as simple as: "invest in inflation-protection bonds." Others are benchmarked against a CPI bogey. However, to a large extent, particularly since the introduction of U.S. Treasury IPBs, the industry is moving towards using indexes of one or more IPBs as a bogey for strategic inflation-protected mandates.

These types of mandates may prove to be an increasingly popular strategy for defined benefit pension plans, whose participants typically receive retirement benefits linked to terminal year wages, and endowments, which are charged with maintaining and improving the quality and quantity of real services delivered to their constituencies.

In the last 15 years, a secular bull market in traditional financial assets has set the tone for investing attitudes. Largely driven by disinflation, returns greatly exceeded inflation and wage increases. If these abnormally high returns begin to slow, as they certainly will, and inflation begins to rise, plan sponsors face the risk of being dangerously underfunded as a result of increasing nominal pension liabilities.

Given IPBs unique ability to provide guaranteed real returns, they have found favor with a variety of financial institutions that have the common goal of maximizing risk adjusted real returns. The underlying asset/liability structure of these organizations creates substantial exposure to the negative consequences of inflation. IPBs are unique in their ability to erase the negative consequences of inflation. Unlike other asset classes that attempt to accomplish this goal, IPBs are simultaneously liquid, contractual in their inflation protection, and have a substantial real yield locked-in to the maturity date.

Tactical Use in Conventional Mandates There are compelling reasons for using IPBs in a tactical manner within existing mandates. Depending on pricing, IPBs can be effectively used as an alternative to short duration fixed-income instruments, or as a way to profit from a bearish view of the prevailing inflation rate environment. Market participants may also feel real interest rates will decline in the future, which will more positively impact IPB than nominal bond prices. Specific short-term trading opportunities, characteristic of many sectors in their early stages of development, have also arisen. These opportunities exist when liquidity and marketplace understanding are rapidly developing. While the benefits of this evolution mainly accrue to the market as a whole, those market participants with the keenest insights and access to the best information are most handsomely rewarded.

In addition to providing another relative value opportunity (as discussed above), IPBs offer an attractive means to dampen portfolio volatility. Since these bonds to some extent hedge against rising interest rates, investment in IPBs allows for investment in other higher returning assets without creating excessive risk when compared to the portfolio's benchmark. As a result, investment managers will no doubt find situations where IPBs offer attractive returns per unit of risk. Without real return histories, the IPBs' correlation and volatility versus other assets are generally modeled using nominal yield data — less inflation as a proxy for real yields — as well as real yield data from other countries' IPB markets. But judgment must reign supreme, since the future will rarely simply mirror the past.

Nevertheless, the advantages of tactical allocations should not be oversold. Prudent active managers will only use tactical IPBs to better achieve the goals mandated via the assigned benchmarks. Sponsors that are seeking inflation protection or growth of purchasing power are best advised to explore explicit strategic allocations to IPB mandates.

Synthetic Real Guaranteed Investment Contracts (GICs)

The guaranteed investment contract (GIC) market has evolved rapidly over the last five years. The latest evolution makes use of IPBs to offer plan participants synthetic real GICs. A definition of a synthetic *real* GIC is in order, but first we should distinguish synthetic GICs from traditional GICs.

A traditional GIC is issued by an insurance company and is a general obligation of the issuer. In contrast, a synthetic GIC represents ownership of a specific diversified portfolios of assets, typically a high quality, low duration bond portfolio. The bond portfolio is "wrapped" by a benefit responsive "book-value wrapper," that allows the beneficiaries to redeem benefits at book value. In this way, synthetic GICs meet the needs of GIC investors. In addition to providing the features of traditional GICs, synthetic GICs provide the additional security of a fully diversified pool of assets backing their value, rather than a single guarantor.

Crediting Rate Formula Participants who invest in synthetic GICs demand relative stability in the crediting rate, but still desire some responsiveness to interest rates. Providers of book value wrappers for synthetic GICs demand low tracking error between the book value and market value of the assets. These dual goals are accomplished by applying the credit rate formula, which defines the crediting rate in terms of the yield and duration of the fixed income portfolio. The synthetic GIC crediting rate formula is:

$$CR = [(MV/BV)^{(1/D)}(1 + YTM)] - 1$$

The interpretation of the crediting rate formula is straightforward.[1] If market value (MV) exceeds book value (BV), the ratio is greater than one, and the portfolio can afford to pay out a crediting rate (CR) that is slightly higher than the portfolio yield (YTM) of the assets. The exponential term $1/D$ is the reciprocal of the portfolio's modified duration. In this way book value will converge to market value. The reason the equation works so well is that changes in market value are normally offset by opposite changes in portfolio yield. The effect of the counteracting phenomena is stable crediting rates.

A synthetic real GIC works the same way; however, it is designed to result in stability of real (inflation-adjusted) principal and interest. Given that real interest rates are less volatile than nominal rates, marking portfolios to market and wrapping them is less onerous than it is for nominal bonds.

Since IPBs are simply bonds for which the price, coupon, and principal are defined in terms of real dollars, the equation can be directly applied to get stable "real" crediting rates. This results in a modification to the formula:

$$CR = CR_r + CR_i$$

$$= [(MV/BV)^{(1/D')} \times (1 + YTM_r) \times (1 + INFL)] - 1$$

A feature of the formula is that the real component of the crediting rate (CR_r) will exhibit the desired stability. Simultaneously, the inflation-linked component (CR_i) will provide an immediate, complete, and highly visible credit to account for reported inflation. The

---

[1] For a more detailed discussion see Edward Rennie, "The Behavior and Market Responsiveness of Synthetic GICs," *Financial Analysts Journal* (September/October 1994).

standard terms are replaced with their corresponding real counter-parts: (D´) real duration, (YTM$_r$) real yield, and (INFL) inflation.

Mutual Funds

Given the convenience, safety, low overhead costs, and access to state-of-the-art "institutional" strategies that mutual funds provide for the institutional and retail marketplace, many investors will choose to invest in IPBs via a mutual fund structure. A mutual fund has the advantage of offering professional management of an aggregated portfolio and thereby direct access to many of the value added strategies outlined above. IPB mutual funds also typically will allow investors to choose between distribution or re-investment of inflation accruals.

Hedge Funds and Partnerships

Hedge funds and partnerships may find that IPBs offer attractive vehicles for expressing their views on future inflation. These speculators[2] will add initial liquidity to the market and will likely ensure that any blatant mispricings of the Treasury auctions do not occur. However, hedge funds are typically setup to have broad-based appeal among risk takers. As such they are usually not tailored to meet the needs of those strategic investors who have specific "inflation protection" or even "real return" goals. In the near term their demand for IPBs would be tactical in nature.

---

[2] The term "speculators" is not pejorative when used by economists. Speculators earn returns by absorbing risk premiums.

Chapter 10

Conclusion

The financial markets are currently enjoying an unprecedented period of falling inflation and high real returns. But the lessons learned thousands of years ago in Mesopotamia and Egypt will be relearned by investors in the future. A secular inflationary environment will no doubt cause substantial losses to those investors caught unprepared. Fortunately, the decision by the U.S. Treasury to issue IPBs provides an attractive vehicle to hedge against this possibility. In fact, the issuance of billions of dollars of these securities will ultimately spawn a whole array of similar securities from both domestic and international issuers.

      The creation of this new asset class is sure to have broad-reaching implications for how both institutional and retail investors structure their portfolios. Soon an allocation to IPBs will be an integral part of an overall asset allocation. Negatively correlated with other asset classes which are inflation sensitive, IPBs increase the efficiency of the overall investment portfolio, allowing for a superior risk/return trade-off which is quite independent of any inflation forecast.

      Development of this market started with a limited number of specialists. Evolution of this market will see heavy participation by mainstream pension funds, foundations, insurance companies, and retail investors, both directly and through mutual fund vehicles. Given the Treasury's determination to issue a sufficient quantity of IPBs to ensure adequate liquidity, the market will be limited only by the degree of understanding of the general investment community. As institutional plan sponsors and their consultants begin to fully appreciate the importance of this asset class, absorption of multi-billion dollar issuance will be easily facilitated. Once the institutional investment community has embraced this asset, the retail channel should be all the more willing to invest.

Issuers will benefit not only from avoiding having to pay the embedded inflation risk premium, but also from superior matching of real assets and real liabilities. Financial innovation and engineering will help every step of the way, creating an array of unique structures and derivative products to more perfectly match issuer and investor preferences. Expanded issuance by corporate and governmental issuers, both domestically and abroad, combined with the creation of derivative instruments will produce a marketplace virtually unrecognizable today.

As institutional and retail clients refine their expectations for IPB investment management firms, these firms will have to display capabilities in a number of essential areas in order to have returns which consistently exceed a relevant benchmark. First, as with any fixed income product, interest rate strategies will be important in determining performance versus a benchmark index. Macroeconomic forecasts which accurately anticipate secular trends in interest rates and the changes to the shape of the yield curve will be one of the key "cylinders" for adding value just as for nominal bond portfolios. Portfolios of IPBs will also involve the added challenge of effectively forecasting real yields. Second, analysis of sovereign international issuers will be required given the opportunities available in these markets. Third, managers will need strong competencies in all of the major U.S. sectors given that IPBs will be issued by a variety of corporate and mortgage issuers. Along with these investments will come proper maintenance of associated currency risk. Fourth, strong analytical resources will be essential for determining relative value in both the underlying and derivative instruments which will be created.

For institutional investors, modern portfolio theory which argues for risk diversification through the purchase of uncorrelated assets will be the initial attraction to this market. The challenge will not be to justify the purchase of these assets using technical measures such as volatility and correlation. These should be relatively self evident. The most difficult hurdle will be to incorporate broader secular scenarios into the analysis. Especially after the heady returns of the 1980s and 1990s, an inflationary world where nominal returns are low and real returns for traditional financial assets are sharply negative seems very distant indeed.

One prominent endowment plan manager struggled with this problem when trying to explain risk in a manner that could be readily understood by his investment board. After his quantitative analysis of volatilities, correlations, standard deviations, and tracking error measures all fell on uninterested ears, he showed the board what happened to the purchasing power, or real value, of the plan during the 1970s. The result was a 30% loss in real terms. He suggested that his challenge was to quantify risk and return in different macro-environments. He wanted them to understand that while he did not expect a replay of the 1970s in the immediate future, this was a scenario that could be used as a metric for downside risk in any broadly diversified asset allocation.

If investors, whether institutional or retail, undertake this type of big picture thinking about their investments, IPBs, fueled by Treasury issuance, will grow in importance beyond the Treasury's most optimistic projections. We firmly believe that an IPB allocation will ultimately become more common than real estate, venture capital, and various other alternative portfolio investments currently being considered by investors. Our hope is that the topics discussed in this book have acted as an effective introduction to one of the most exciting new development in the U.S. investment arena in many years.

Appendix

Mexico's Tesobonos

The historical episode best illustrating the credit distinction between domestic currency debt, domestic index-linked debt, and foreign denominated debt is the Mexican peso crisis of December 1994.

Tesobonos were Treasury bills issued by the United Mexican States denominated in nuevo pesos but indexed to the exchange rate. Although they were not inflation indexed, they had many of the characteristics of inflation-indexed debt, including a much lower interest rate than non-indexed peso debt. Because of their unique structure, the Mexican government could not "print" its way out of a liquidity problem. Any laxness in monetary policy would be reflected in a weaker peso exchange rate and a greater Tesobonos obligation.

The investment community, and the Mexican government, did not anticipate the fragility of the situation. Mexico had come to be quite dependent on foreign capital, and the issuance under the Tesobonos program created U.S. $30 billion of new outstandings during the second half of 1994.

Some shrewd observers may have anticipated the problems and exchanged their pesos for dollars, initiating pressure. The Mexican authorities, it seems, exacerbated the situation by mandating that Mexican banks cease their highly profitable practice of financing peso assets with dollar liabilities. As 1994 evolved, pressure on the exchange rate began to build.

By December of 1994 Mexico had spent virtually all of its foreign exchange reserves in an attempt to defend its "crawling band" exchange rate policy. When the band actually broke, holders of dollar-denominated Brady bonds and dollar-indexed Tesobonos were insulated from the currency devaluation. However, because of the substantial size of these positions, and the fact that the value of them, in terms of pesos, grew larger with each downward tick in the value of the currency, market participants simultaneously started to assess a higher default premium against this Mexican debt to account for increased credit risk. This adversely fed back and created additional pressure on the exchange rate. The exchange rate depreciated far more than anyone anticipated. Mexico was perceived by many to be on the edge of financial collapse. The stress spilled into neighboring countries. Soon the problem was global in proportion.

Ultimately, all holders of Tesobonos received their fully indexed principal and interest. The peso value of this was dramatically increased by the indexation. Since Mexico avoided default, dollar-based investors received exactly the dollar-based return the Tesobonos originally promised. In contrast, the holders of non-indexed peso denominated debt suffered the impact of a currency devaluation, from 3.40 pesos per dollar to 6.80 pesos per dollar, which reduced their (dollar-based) maturity proceeds by 50%.

What this episode highlighted is that indexed securities issued by sovereigns, such as Tesobonos and IPBs, are legally domestic currency instruments, but from a risk and safety perspective largely mimic foreign currency instruments.

Index